WAVELENGTHS

First published by Holland House Editions
52 Val Plaisant, St Helier, Jersey, JE2 4TB

ISBN 978-0-9568865-0-7 (paperback)
Copyright © the authors

A CIP catalogue reference for this book is available in the
British Library.

Design by Webb & Webb Design Limited
www.webbandwebb.co.uk
Cover illustration by Alastair Best
Type set in Eric Gill's Joanna and Gill Sans
Printed by Manor Creative, Eastbourne, UK

New poetry in the Channel Islands

WAVELENGTHS

chosen by ALASTAIR BEST & LINDA ROSE PARKES

HOLLAND HOUSE *editions*

CONTENTS

ROBERT JAMES ANDERSON

House-Call Version 2.1

Condensed like milk in retrospect
the trajectory of
first steps along the promenade
to last steps home
seems
brief
as a raindrop.

I had wanted your golden skin
for a croissant in the morning

Ten-thirty in the Twenty-First Century
and the hairstyles are high

I cannot explain you
and it would be crass to try and do so

Just a little guilt
can help immeasurably.

ALASTAIR BEST

La Maison Maret revisited

It's someone else's now;
But then it was the place I'd come from.
The yew trees are still there,
Just as they were in 1945:
Concentric, poodle-clipped,
Aloof in British racing green.

On Sunday mornings
The Reverend RJ Hibbs MA (Oxon)
Would park his Raleigh by the gate
And, sorting through his pile of 78s,
Play us the bells from Trinity steeple.
Down in the yard you'd hear
The needle's exalted hiss.

We drank immoderately –
Vimto, ice cream soda, Cherry Ciderette –
And smoked in houses made from bales of hay.

One day a cow died. It took
Four men, in pouring rain,
To haul her through a trail of blood and piss.

On summer nights, I found it hard to sleep
Owing to my fear of snakes.
(Beneath the bedsprings, the Black Mamba,
Deadliest snake in all Africa
Lay coiled and waiting).
When I switched the light on
The moths would come:
Hostile, furred projectiles which would
Ricochet against the lampshade or

Crash land on the counterpane stunned,
Still menacing, their wings vibrating like midget fighters.

The airing cupboard was my sanctuary –
A Switzerland of calm and folded blankness:
I came to love the smell of ironing.

Dégringolade

Takes the floor assured.
Cockney; whistling;
Gait a sturdy amble;
Cap rakish; bum jut
By chimp suit accentuated;
Tie off target, then
The uneven paving stone,
The banana skin glissade.
Punctuated, derailed,
A collapsed puppet, he
Cascades floorwards, paws
The air, pleading;
Capsizes
In a soundless cry of pain.

Paeonies

Are absurd. Loaded with such stuff
Surely the tree is unequal to its task?
How can so frail a scaffold
Support all this?
Each year's flowers, fist-sized,
Take us unaware.
Is it the bigness,
The extravagance, or perhaps
The unapologetic way
They just one day arrive?
Crimson suits them.
They sit, couched on indented leaves,
As fat as emperors, and just as insecure.
We know it can't go on.
Within a week, deposed, their glorious taffeta
Is stripped and scattered; while the tree,
Relieved of its imperial cargo,
With straightened limbs,
Grows calmly on.

Follow the links
after WH Auden

Hedda Gabler leaves the stage
Brandishing a loaded gun;
Unfolds her copy of the Sun
Evaluates the city page.

Hostile polyps overrun
The gastro-intestinal tract;
Horses that the bookies backed
Canter home at ten to one.

Schoolboys con their German verbs;
Middle income ladies swoon
Over hard-backed novels, soon
Stiletto heels patrol the kerbs.

Drenched by equinoctial rains
Those are pearls that were her eyes;
Anger management applies
When travelling on suburban trains.

Sunsets of a roseate hue
Pierce the Hebridean mists;
Female watercolourists
Flood their skies with cobalt blue.

Superparasitic worms
Exercise their mystic powers
Devouring, in Martello towers
The secret files of bankrupt firms.

Memo to the Jersey Milk Marketing Board

Poets are mysteriously silent on the subject of cheese GK CHESTERTON

What inspiration pure, divine
Unutterably noble, fine
Invented CHEESE, most blessed dish
Successor to both meat and fish.
We, who are martyrs to our pud
Eat much less of it than we should
(For baser instincts, as a rule
Prefer to play the rhubarb fool,
And when left to their devices
Will trifle with meringues and ices).
So as we guzzle Windsor Soup,
Or Parma ham and canteloup
We should reserve a space somewhere
For Parmesan and Camembert
And Munster, Lancashire and Brie
And handmade Cheddar, Caerphilly.
Why should our blunted tastebuds shun
That epic work of man – Stilton?
Does life afford a nobler view
Than sumptuous squares of Port Salut?
And why deprive the ardent molar
That yearns to nibble Gorgonzola?
Begone dull puddings, give us instead
That inseparable friend of bread
That boon companion of wine –
Beloved CHEESE; and let us dine
On all these lactic miracles divine.
And let us thank our friends the French
Whose cheeses have a wondrous stench
Thanks to their repudiation
Of every EU regulation.
That being said, there's nothing deader
Than supermarket Jersey cheddar.

lost

borne by the waves
he was
so lost how long
he had forgotten
long so long in the water
light hope
brilliant all day gone now
borne away by the waves
lost so long lost so
empty the distance
soon now
the darkness the water
so gentle
he was
soon
borne away
by the waves
and lost
in darkness and
distance

SHARON CHAMPION

Tea with Grand-mère

She stoops, dove-gentle caresses my hand,
Guides me along the path
In powder puff slippers,
Her flowery pinafore billowing
In the spick and span breeze.

In Meltonian white sandals
I jump over the cracks
Of the crazy paving
Where the dragon might eat me –
Tugging her arm we zig-zag
Through the maze of Burgundy
Sweet Williams and Shock Pink Snapdragons –

I poke my finger in their mouth,
Daring their fire …
Now sniff the Stock, Pale Blue and Lilac –
This is her smell …

Precise fingers pull some weeds,
Then hand me a Puff Dandelion
'One o'clock, two o'clock, three o'clock …'
Seed helicopters scatter and dance
Propelled by my breath.

Allez, lavez les mains avant manger.

Boiled ham, Jersey tomatoes, steamed beetroot
And buttered bread, a sliced two-pounder,

Home delivered by Bird's Bakery.
The shiny wax paper traces
My finger down its blue stripes.
Perched on my embroidered cushion
I reach across the Mahogany table
For plump peaches, scoop them
With the glistering silver spoon.

Grand-mère smiles her cornflower eyes,
Pours glubs of cream.

A Tumble-turn

I want straight and smooth and
a swimsuit like hers, navy bri-nylon
with fluted skirt trim that fans as she skips,
is taut and clingy – not like my sag-bag red one.

Susan, in the marzipan cove, with her pig-tails –
mine a pony of jealous curls.
Susan is busy bucket and spading, mum unravelling
mohair wool for my powder blue bolero.

Dad huffs 'n' puffs into the black tube
of the faded canvas lilo,
his eyes popping like those pin-balls at Funland.

We drag his hot air over cockle and whelk shells,
ouching past rocks, basking like crocs they lie in wait
festooned in limpets and creepy bloodsuckers,

quick-dip our toes into cool salt, wade out as dad
chucks the green airbed, I am waist deep,
belly flop onto the warm inflated tubes,
dangle sea-fingers, float ...

dad spins me – whoosh, the lilo a dark shadow above my head
murky-swirl-clouds, woolly ears, foam bubbles up my nose,
eyes panic open ... eyes panic closed

I know I'm drowning

hair tendrils shroud my face
the darkness smothers ...

dad's arm as he umbrellas me, anchors me
choking-coughing-burping, hair in rats' tails

I've lost my scarlet ribbon … what will mum say?

My costume decorated with maroon and brown vraic
I sog up the beach, a sea-monster biting its lip,
mum waves her knitting:

I'm getting on like a house on fire

Susan is bucket and spading, all dry and warm and neat
with quiet hair and a perfect sandcastle

– and I hate her

The Tainted Perfume of my Mother's Breasts

She wets her finger,
Twirls ringlets in my damp hair,
Brushes it with a stocking 'for shine',
Tender soaks her pungence –
Lilies of the valley, wild lavender perfume her breasts,
Cocooned in her scent I am lulled to their rampant secret.

Mum smiles electric,
Dad glints as he grabs, twirls her;
She giggles like a young girl
In silk petticoat peeps –
Then breaks away to check her Yorkshire puds
Risen like top hats.
Queen of the Sunday roast,
Her homely rump sustains.

Olga loves Bob, his carpenter's hands,
His sawdust smell, kitchen cupboards painted proud,
In Emerald Courtelle she presides, drinks tea with her sisters,
Their lips scorched with gossip,

Beryl's three months gone an' he's run off
                              – the swine!

She rests her 'fresh-as-a-mountain-stream' cigarette
In the rainbow belly of the ormer shell,
My benign mother-of-pearl picks up the steel needles –
Knit one, crossover yarns stitch Fair Isle –
Sherbert Lemon and Turquoise for me,
For Dad she swaps to chunky 4ply,
Bottle green wool inches like a slow worm …

A fisherman's jumper to keep him warm on the breakwater.

Later, in a wisp of Elnett hairspray,
Her lips petalled by Coty No. 7 'Soft Rose,'
She scuttles up Sand Street in duster coat swirl …

Precious Olga … at 47 placed in an ash casket.

The Spirit Level

Shavings fly, dance, curl,
I pick them up
put them in my pocket –
sea-horse ringlets
to play with …

Stooped in his workshop in his sailor blue overalls,
he planes the wood, rubs rough fingers against its grain,
plucks his lead pencil from behind his ear,
marks mortices and tenons, squares with his chisel
so they fit like a jigsaw, then

saws the serrated shark teeth;
he smoothes the deal again with his plane,
coaxes a Norwegian forest to yield gentle
for sanding. A burny smell …

He reaches into his toolbag for silver hammer and nail;
fist-taps over fingers. Married to his precise hands
their combined heat gleams,
transforms splintered planks.

He turns that final screw
then checks the equilibrium –
yellow air bubble central in the window
of his spirit level.

But now I stroke your right hand,
speak to your fingers –

grab my fist Dad,
Thor-hammer clench it.

Tools are quiet now:
neat rows
in the cupboard
under the stairs.

SIMON CROWCROFT

Compulsory Showers

The boy and the girl in the naked crowd
knew each other from swimming classes.
Once, frog-kicking past each other slowly,
(he had not mastered the crawl like his bronzed peers)
her instep was swept by his heel, and he apologised;
they had sat by the pool-side: she wanted
to play in an orchestra; he would become a doctor.

True, they had day-dreamed, he more than she:
the baring of her breasts, the colour of her bush – it *was* black,
but her shaven head was not in his scheme of things;
his hair had always been short, but for a girl
whose fancy dared go no further than a kiss,
it was a shock to see his genitals.

Luckily the male queue flowed faster:
he saw a boy with a crimson face
trying to hide his erection;
she saw the divided husbands
and wives, exchanging encouraging words,
twisting bright rings in their grooves.

Coup

He's dead, I heard at breakfast; by lunchtime
the present tenses had been rounded up and shot;
I couldn't say at dusk, my father works abroad,
owes me a letter, or that he does anything.
The future tenses, his 'wills', his 'going to 's', have fled
dropping promises behind them, and in the squares
the second person pronoun wars against the third,
addressing the dead as if alive, as if listening,
at last, to my language – 'I love you'
scrawled like graffiti in the occupied streets.
For the past holds the town, it always did:
he taught me to keep still when watching animals;
he used to pull back my shoulders to correct
this stoop; he left home when I was ten.

Crutches

Remember the first yards across the ward's
miles of polished lino, crutches akimbo,
and silvered in the slanting sun,
the exercise as impossible
as crossing a falls?

Then some expert would swing by,
I'd say, 'You'll be like that, pretty soon' –
'Never!' you'd scowl,
flinging the crutches down,
getting your burning leg horizontal.

And the sweating physiotherapist –
remember how he kept leaving off
your torture to mop his face,
how the pools of his perspiration
impeded your progress?

Like overdue books, for months
they were left in the hall, save when
you machine-gunned your brothers with them,
or took trips around the uneven yard
for old times' sake.

Incident in Liberation Square

Thierry's the one with the wide smile, perfect teeth
and diseased heart, who leaves his books on his desk
(*Advanced Learner's Dictionary, A Modern Grammar,
Cambridge English for Holiday Courses*)

not because he's idle but to avoid their combined weight
on the short walk back, where the host-family I selected
pampers him with low-fat, low-salt, low-sugar meals
and a complete absence of stairs.

We handle him like a single long-stemmed glass
among tumblers, would bubble-wrap him, or place staff
on all sides like police outriders, but to his peers,
forgetful of Monday's briefing, he's just a student:

they jostle past him in the corridor, muss his hair,
land soft punches on his shoulder; when he comes to the office
to quiz me about the zoo trip, there's a Polish girl
on each side, their arms draped lovingly around his neck.

He likes it here – likes the sea, where he floats,
grinning back at the sun, or goes gingerly into the surf;
likes the young German who offers him her towel,
eyeing his scars, a top Parisian surgeon's handiwork;

likes our Liberation Square, where on Friday he walks
with the girls, talks in four languages, and is assaulted:
head-butted, kicked in the face, the ribs, the groin;
'French scum!' my compatriots call him, kicking on.

Exeats

The red tail-lights would narrow, brightening
at the junction with the high road, then out of sight,
and we turned once more to the boarding-house.

Another wet weekend in Salisbury, Bournemouth
or Christchurch, our father catching up on British papers
or trying the patience of drunks – they only stopped him

for a bob, but his stories of an alcoholic father
and 'new starts' would leave their throats drier than ever.
At awkward and expensive mealtimes he advised us

about our 'hormones', whatever they were. Feelings
harboured for a girl glimpsed across the chapel,
were these the same chemicals in the blood that,

excepting exeats, had orphaned us? Praying myself to sleep
I dreamed god's house was a dormitory of girls,
though holding hands was banned, and praying together

the closest I would ever get to ecstasy.
Neither my father, his head buried in a book,
nor his surrogate in the skies, had much to say about that.

Winter Sunday evenings remind me of him;
I am wondering where he is on the London Road.
Clouds sweeping in from America rain on me.

Rocquaine Mermaid

She heaved herself up on a barnacled rock;
sea-water broke from her sun-blonde hair
down over shoulders, freckled with salt:
a broad-breasted kelpy
launched from bright water.

No seal she: nor odd fish either,
but strangeness enough
in her queer duality.
Something feral
in those luminous eyes, some leonine thing
in the strong, broad face
turning, in sunlight,
to Lihou, Fort Grey.

Trapped
in triangular space,
among moonscape rocks, sea-wall, sky,
too close to shore or for comfort;
misplaced, adrift
in a place unfamiliar,
she saw me, heron-still
in chill water, staring, staring

and slid like a seal, soundlessly, smoothly,
into the rising tide's rich, sweet sanctuary,

leaving me,
human me, her shore-bound kin,
two-legged, bereft, breather of air,
with a longing to hold her, inhale
her salt skin,
to fill my rough hands with wet fistfuls of hair.

CAROL GAUDION

Henry's Last Katherine

A shaft of sunlight kisses me awake.
I am alone in my great bed, the dream
I'm tasting is of Thomas Seymour.
This is treason and I shiver, though the room
With the summer sun is warming up.
From the sheets rise the smell of roses.
When Henry sleeps here they stink,
They reek of pus and aged sweat.
Sufficient unto the day is the evil thereof.
My ladies are entering in a swish of robes.
I shall chase away the demons
Of beheaded queens in the plushness
Of my crimson dress, the flashing
Of rubies and diamonds, heavy
Against my white childish breasts.

The day is for dressing, the night for disrobing.
All times are for prayer.

At night my ladies bring out with a snicker
The black lace nightgown I've ordered
To keep my old king's lust alive.
I shake amongst the candles.
Prayer fails me.

MARTIN GREENE

Eels

You break into my sleep,
Like a long breeze across the roughing surface of the loch,
An old story of eels you say, brought for the telling.
You delve into my dream sack of what is and what is not,
Thrusting fingers into brackish bogs, your lilting brogue, the dark,
ditch waters of your Irish past.

Born between the wars,
Between the alms house and the beggar amputees,
Your father's comrades at the Somme, the screaming torment of
his dreams.
Then quiet moments by the loch, running errands for your Ma,
The burnished boots of 'prentice boys, orange-sashed, the
bristling rattle of their Lambeg drums, your tattooed harp,
the problematic of that internecine brawl.

You stretch the membrane of those moments taut,
Its surface snaps, your memory twists like elvers writhing in some
frozen bog,
Their cold below-ness, your storyteller's knack,
Its gift as deep as peat, its holy need to breath the rhythm of
your tribe,
The river's undulating beat.

Sure McGrath, and the 'wee fella', who could swim the loch,
Your second cousin and those other lads,
Drowned in the waters off Narvik, trapped in the twisted frame
of that shuddering hulk, calling you back, 'Billy c'mon',
I saw your tears arrange themselves in perfect drops,
We held our breath and watched the silent archive footage fade
to black.

Now that distance fills with myth,
And with each dying breath your first-born son wrings his
thinning fingers,
I rub your bones inside his flesh, and curl his hand into a fist and
remember standing by the Thames,
That same hand holding mine, reading out their names for fear of
leaving them unread, those 20 000 men the wolf packs left behind.

Like eels submerged, clinging to the bottom of the loch,
Where memory preserves,
You gather up each word and put it gently back,
'Some other time', you say, 'I'll tell you more about that world'.

JULIETTE HART

Thief

I tried to take your breath last night
waited
thick in the dark
until you slept
fingered your spine
shunted my knees
so you turned

then under the bellow of quilt
matched
your inhale
exhale
until
shallow
guttered

tonight I was lulled by dusk
when your hand
palmed my belly
I took the hum
of your breath
on the cusp
of my tongue

Solemate

On top of a wardrobe
an album opens
onto a creamy girl
tucked into satin
and silver sandals.

She's looking
at the boy
not the camera.
Back then he lifted
her more than stilettos.

There were summer
lunches on benches
with flip-flops slipped off
and winter evenings with
cashmere socks paired

on the sofa.
House hunting in rain,
tights damp in boots,
she still kept pace
with his size twelves.

But the last kick she had
was from finding
cerise pumps
in a half price sale.
For dancing.

The pull of leather
alive in the twist
of cord in her hand, looped
between eyelets,
already starting to fray.

The Salmon Coat

It's over a century since these thirty fish
                        lost their struggle
                of eddying existence
near Vladivostok.

Trawled from the Lower Amur
they gulped their last,
were gutted to the rush of river
and pulse of open fire.

Perhaps pelt-wrapped hunters supped
rye vodka, slept well that night,
or took a tea of boiled ginseng
to help them home.

What gifts then for their women:
the scraped skins to be sewn with sinew,
painted side panels stitched with silk
into patterns of tigers or shaman spirits.

Now slotted on a pole in a cabinet,
this coat of sixty sides
of salmon is muted in moss,
coral and ghost terracotta.

Lacking metal buttons and leather loops,
stifled in a glass tank, exhibit 626-1905
hangs unlined, unfinished,
                                unworn.

A Verdun Veteran

He was nine
when his father
saw his cat jump
onto the kitchen table
one time too many;

made him tie it
in a sack
with a brick,
drop it into
the water butt;

he returned
and saw the bubbles
still rising.

That afternoon,
the two crouched
side by side
in the allotment
cropping strawberries;

his father pinching
the stalks
with thumbnail,
an inch above
the fruit,

to avoid touching
and bruising
its flesh.

A Single Returns on the Gatwick Express

A rush-dash thrum mesmerises
until the suck
of an opposing train raises
dried eyes:

nearside trees dart fleeter
than pebble-dashed Tudor
Purley
PurleyOaks
conservatories
cecking
dead glass
cracked grass
plastic chairs brittle on slabs
holes stashed in shed backs
SouthCroydon
brick boxes
steel wedges
tattoos tagged on walls and bridges
WandsworthCommon
guy jogging dodges dog shit
caned allotments
footie pitch
ClaphamJunction
dirty-nosed terraces leer
plastic bags mashed in leaves
pallet boards tangle buddleia
Rubbish Clearance a sign pleads
BatterseaPark
graffiti webbed
Thames ebbs

Time to cluster baggage and brace
for a stripped flat
Clock a quiet sticker in top left
of 2nd class pane:
a black dot centred and the invitation
BREAK HERE

Q.E.D.

We lay beached
on the soft sand dune of my bed.
I looked with such pleasure
at the beautiful geometric shape
of your body and wished I could draw
to keep this image always clear:
eyes closed, head on shoulder,
mouth gentle, the strong
brown arms and legs making a triangle
of male strength. Strong chest
densely haired in pewter haze,
curved solid hard belly, strong thighs, one knee raised.
I could have measured
all these curves, arcs and angles,
attempted to replicate this man
whose body had given me such pleasure.
But a drawing or a sculpture would not
assure me of your pleasure in me,
speak to me, tease me, touch me.

ALAN JONES

Still Life without Herring

After 1629 Willem Heda never included a herring in his pictures
OXFORD COMPANION TO ART

Too late for your
Haarlem breakfast:
the cat's dragged the pewter plate
     precariously
onto the table's edge,
and anyway the oysters
are starting to smell.
There must be flies circling the crab
and the pudding has been wrecked,
the blackberry pie-case a bloodied shell.
The lemon with the spiralling peel
has shrivelled among the debris
of cracked hazels and walnuts
near the knife with the shining blade.
The ham still looks tasty,
if you want to risk it,
and there's a half-eaten mince pie
by the upturned Venetian goblet.
But,
looking on the bright side,
it's after 1629,
so, thankfully, the herring
has been replaced by a lobster.
No need to be deterred,
is there,
by the snuffed out candle
in the dark background?

Flying Westward into Perth

From this height
we can view the Dreamtime canvas,
see everywhere the dark stipple of spinifex,
ribbed in contoured undulations,
peppering the rusty ochre.
Palette pools of lime and clay,
ash mixed with oil, fleck the umber.
Abandoned, dried serpentine skins lace the valleys,
barbed kangaroo prints edge the crusted saltpan smears,
lizard estuaries encroach into land,
white sickles of sand-dunes –
witchetty grubs squirming in carved bowls
near women squatting in flamed dust.
And always, those concentric circles of rest.

Hidden messages for those free to
walk about.

But over every surface
the graffiti of man-tracks
cobweb the canvas.
Tangram intersections
scar the print,
undeviating ruled lines
disappear into misted edges,
and, eventually,
jarring turquoise geometry
violates the tints
of crushed rock.

Our own charcoal shadow
scrawls another defacement.

We approach the airport and
the angularity of modern abstract,
land, unswerving,
on soiled white dashes
stretching straight into the horizon.

Ninety Mile Beach

A daily two-mile jog
northwards to nowhere
across featureless sands,
crashing breakers on her left,
smothering sand-dunes to her right –

and two miles back again
into the same unforgiving wind
that had covered his footprints
on that first night alone.

The blankness of the sand
appalled her, the only marker
a rotting eyeless grouper,
rib-cage picked clean
by the bickering gulls.

More difficult now each day
to prod the old dog into joining her.
Only eighty-eight miles
to go, she joked, following
a quad-bike's mazy pattern
through the seabirds
jabbing at flounders
in the draining froth.

She knew there was a lighthouse
at the end of it all – close to
that salt-blasted, blood-red tree,
amongst whose roots, they said,
the spirits waved goodbye.

Here, in these empty two miles,
they had noticed things together:
the bleached driftwood root
moulded like a seven-legged octopus,
those infinitely varied clam shells,
always unhinged, single,

the dried grass heads they called
tumbleweeds
spinning unfailingly northwards.

She bent, released one from a clump
of dried wrack,
sent it rolling on its way.

32 Pearson Park, Hull

'This was Mr Larkin's room. He stayed
The whole time he was at the Library, till
They moved him.' Chilling green ceiling, pale cream
Walls and those high windows Mrs Noakes found
Difficult to clean; a safe eyrie, where,
Binoculars in hand, he swooped on life
Below – noted mini-skirted schoolgirls,
Tramps deep in litter baskets in the park
While Queen Victoria frowned through chestnut
Clumps and ageing couples bent together on
The bowling green by the lobelia bed.

'Mr Larkin made this flat almost his own.'
Uncomfortable chintzy armchairs,
Wide, old-fashioned metal bed, books, records
Of Bechet, Basie, Oliver and blues
Played on his Pye Black Box gramophone
To drown the jabbering Duffins from below
And their squeaking daughter he hungered
To cudgel or tear-gas bomb down the chimney.

But if he lay and soaked and saw the bathroom
Montage on the wall through steamy haze –
Blake's Vision of Body and South with the
Punch cartoon pantomime horse pulling
In both directions – did he feel, at last,
He had found the answer: a home so sad
That masked and mirrored those other places
Where he didn't feel at home, those awful
Christmases in Coventry with mother
and hotel rooms with Monica in Sark?

A sombre, siege-defence against invading
Change, far out of reach to all but the rare
Invited guest, who might be honoured with
The dry lettuce sandwich, that he assured them,
Was the speciality of the house.

CHRISTINE JOURNEAUX

Between the Pages

A father leaned back
in his easy chair
to eat an orange,
tore the loose nubbley skin,
and prised apart
the firm pulp inside,
droplets of aromatic juice
staining the local paper
in his lap —

and he remembered
next day
to roll the paper tightly
in a brown wrapper
and send it to his daughter
in some other land

where she sat
under an olive tree
to read it,
the scented pages
unlocking the memory
of a rosewood Buddha lamp
lighting the newspaper
in her father's hands.

Dancing at the Castle

In daylight the castle was a jagged shell
a secret on this side
except for the window of the Great Hall
where a tracery of conifer branches
criss-crossed the void –

        but last night
        I saw a string of riders
        climb the rough track
        to the middle ward
        some carried colours
        of blue and gold
        some stooped heavy
        over their Flemish horses
        crushing the steep bank
        of thyme and rosemary
        shadowy figures danced
        in the glow of the window
        to the sound of lute and harp
and in daylight the castle is a jagged shell
a secret on this side
except for the window of the Great Hall
where a tracery of conifer branches
criss-cross the void.

Almost Letting Go

After a string
of busy shops
the highway softened
into parkland
where beech trees
shaded the hot road,

olive-grey trunks
branched into
fragile sprays
of glossy leaves
floating over
dry stone walls –
almost brushing my face
as the wind rushed
past my ears;

hands hovering
over brakes
when I flew down
Headington Hill
in the silence of
the fifties.

Watching Water-boatmen

Caged in a top-floor flat
noses squashed against
double-glazing
they scan the map of
identical streets
ponderous houses
made to measure gardens

and remember
a potholed farm road
dog-rose hedges
honeyed cornfields
and the secret place
where they'd sat
on a homemade raft
with cucumber sandwiches
watching water-boatmen
row across the pond.

The Wood-carver

They came to 'relocate' him –
the German prisoner of war –
in the middle of the day

and at the foot of a haystack
where the loosed straw
scratched their bare legs
two children nestled
against their older sister –
watched the tears
darken her red shirt –
too young to understand.

That night, soothed by
tales of a magic lamp
they slept, and while their father
talked to his daughter
the wind blew the first leaves
of autumn from the apple tree
outside the kitchen window.

Next morning, on a bale of straw
in the sweet scented barn
they found the carved bird
the man had promised;
its wings of coloured spills
spread in flight.

Warsaw 1942

Mother and child sit
on the ice-covered bench
her arm crooked tight around
his skinny shoulders.
His hand clasps hers;
beneath his dangled feet
two pigeons peck the snow
for specks of grain.

Dzien dobry, the watchman begins,
his breath-haze clouding
the space between them.
No turn of their heads
at the man's approach,
though the birds fly up
to the branches of a linden tree.

The wideness of their eyes amazes him,
huge opals set above high cheek-bones,
their thin skin, blue-tinged alabaster.
Around their faces, emptiness
hums in the brittle air,
too clear and undisturbed.
Their stiff coats glisten with frost.

Shock Treatment

He had slept all night on the open deck,
pitched and tossed across the Channel
from Weymouth, past the Minquiers
and home,
waking once to spew Guinness
over the side, drifted off again,
mouth wide open to the gale.

Landfall, and he drags his familiar scent
of beer and vomit up the hall,
into our kitchen where it clings
to curtains, carpet, hair.

He lays the fruits of therapy on the table:
four paint-by-number canvases –
a rural scene, The Laughing Cavalier,
roe deer in a sunlit glade, and his favourite –
boats moored in a Cornish harbour,
with one small craft nudging
out to sea.

It took five nurses to hold me down
when they gave me the shocks,
he tells us proudly.
I dare not wonder what he means.

Later, mother cannot hang his pictures on the wall –
someone may ask who painted them,
and when,
and where.

Next day the wind has dropped.
He drags the yellow dinghy down the beach
a drunken sailor heading out to sea
heedless of currents, swell or undertow
a bobbing dab of red paint,

rowing away.

Northern Counties School for the Deaf

You ran
and cupped your hands before me
hoping to gather
in your palms
the sound of my laughter
and feel in them my joy:
but your hands felt
nothing
a tiny breath
almost nothing.

You stood
and stared wide-eyed beside me
thinking to catch in a stare
the sound of my words
and find in them my love:
but your eyes heard
nothing
a faint rustle
almost nothing.

You have made God small
after R. S. Thomas

You have made God small
so small I cannot see Him
even the tiniest glimpse
of His shirt-tails eludes me.

You have made Him so small
I cannot feel the warm breeze
fanned up by His feet as
He hurries past along the road.

You have made God so small
and He has been shrinking daily
since His huge frame filled my house
pretending He would protect me.

I have made Him small
so small I do not miss Him
like that other father, full of promises
he did not intend to keep.

In Paris

This year
with only a glimpse
of an Indian moment,
when vapour-
infused light held
the city motionless
summer unravelled
into winter
and in the Tuileries
the wind cut icy
down avenues
of yellowing
plane trees
blew high
the flat indented
leaves from
docked branches
so they drifted
stiff sails down
on flurries of children
running, colliding
arms flung out,
pages turning
to the year's end

Antiphony

We dance together,
she and I,
sidelong glances
measuring our proximities.

She, with her angel wings,
 – fevered and urgent –
is the treble in the partnership.
I hold the crashing bass chords,

sustain her castles in the air.
Forever restless she chases
 – questions – with notes

 so high they pierce the skin,
    plant
needles in the brain.

We play at hide and seek,
collide in discordancies
    to fly apart,
play cat-falls on a razor's edge.

Closing Time

And so they stand
two figures like effigies,
stripped and scoured,
as, silent at the window,
they watch the early petals
whipped from trees
by icy blasts, sleeting
    tears to ground,

A waste, such a waste,
she murmurs, but to herself.

'*The wind **is** chilly*',
her husband rubs
the weeping glass.
Turning, his eyes are
                arrows:
You shafted me,
    he says.

What are you doing out of bed?
The voice, a pistol shot; and she,
flinching through paper skin, is
for a moment, a gazelle poised
                for flight.

But where on earth
    to fly?

She is seized, propelled deftly
backwards and imprisoned
between sheets of blinding
linen. Eyes right, she sees
her husband-ghost has gone –
    to heaven?

She thinks not.

Shafted, shafted;
what kind of word is that?
Fighting sheets, she moves
resentfully, opens wide
her ancient legs; and looks
beyond the sound-proofed
glass where wind-blown flights
of this and that are shreds
    of memory.

Unheard and tuneless,
she hums her refrain:
Brother for brother, one
a bloody awful husband,
the other, his twin, her lover.

What harm was there in that?
her smile curves cheekbones,
under eyes sparking with fever.

Her heated head conjures up,
somewhat crooked, the lover
lost to fortune inventing
soapy powders for cleaner washes.
Her thoughts float and burst,
sudsy bubbles riding high.

Long ago, and long ago,
they had met at a sea-side fair
somewhere green and gold
under massing clouds, each
seeing the other sugar-screened
through a blur of candy-floss,

her eyes on him bluer
than a jay's wing. Unthinking,
he had lifted a hand to her cheek
faintly shadowed with colour.
But his gaze had been intent
on her foaming hair.

He always did like froth.
Her words are sighs
into overheated air
as her lover's son smoothes
the creases of her loss,
with a hand that stirs
                   her sliding heart.

NICKY MESCH

Testing her Metal

But he could be gentle –
the night he turned her
an inch at a time, painstakingly
slotting the panels of her skirt,
the muscled serpent on his arm
lapping salt as he tightened
the unfamiliar studs at her waist,
oiled her shiny new joints,
buffed the cones
on her breastplate
to a blush.

She shuddered at the glint
spilling from his calloused hands –
waist-length wiry coils,
curly copper lashes,
perfect O for a mouth –
and tried to catch her breath
but already he was easing
metal around her head
and welding it in place.

Death of a Unicorn

He almost let her touch him once –
too intent on the scent of the ruby-trimmed cloak
dewing on the grass – her fingers
a horn's breadth from his burr-tangled mane
when he snickered and sidestepped away.

Even a desiccated virgin might tire
of waiting, choose instead to smudge ugliness
with smoky candlelight and rough wine.
Perhaps she'll catch a burly sailor's eye
in a quayside tavern, follow him
into a narrow alley, where she'll pretend
his rum-soaked bristles reek of fresh grazed grass
and the shimmer on his coat isn't the rust
of one hundred fishhooks.

Easier to flee, through crooked streets,
over the bridge – past the ruby-crusted castle
her sister married into – stumbling
and crashing, brambles tearing her skirts,
roots tripping her silk slippers,
until she falls headfirst and heaving
into the hollow at the clearing's edge.

Let this be the night he comes to her,
kneels at her feet, places his muzzle
in her lap. Let him breathe hot
and moist on her skin.

If she raises her eyes she'll find
the image full flesh in front of her –
unicorn and ruby-ringed slut rutting
in a blade of moonlight.

The following twilight she'll return
stained with her sister's scent.
Shivering in a blood-trimmed cloak,
she'll cling to shadow
at the edge of the clearing
and wait.

The Changeling

they can make her
latch it to her breast
until it drains her
to bone

they can make her
dress it in the outfits
she'd bought for him,
its scaly skin scratching
soft blue

they can even make her
take it with her
when she leaves

checking daily
she hasn't slipped back
to wall-staring
while it yowls
out of sight

but they can't stop her
scouring the streets,
peering into car-seats,
buggies and the arms
of every baby-carrier
until she finds him

and when she does find him —
because she *will* find him —
they won't be able
to stop her from doing
what was done to her —

she'll snatch her baby and hurry away,
leaving a demon in his place.

Monster Fruit

I fade into a doorway
at the sight of him
my first, very nearly last —
thighs sticking
to his black leather sofa
hi-fi taking up half the room
Swiss cheese plant
taking over the other
the bulldozing weight
of his promise —
perforated
heart-shaped leaves
leathery and lush
brushing the ceiling
the urge to climb it
out of one world
into another
where a goose
lays golden eggs
a harp plucks
her own strings
and a giant
with hands
too huge
for hooks or zips
might well
fee-fi-fo-fum
at the smell
of blood
and threaten
to grind bone
to make bread

but would
never stoop
to duping a girl
with a promise
to be gentle

A Good Woman

Any woman knows to lock herself
behind a strong door when the ice demon
threatens from the north

but if she's caught unaware
in the bleak dawn after fraught vigil
at the old pastor's bedside

hurrying her steps at the thought
of three small boys tucked home
safe if her man had no coin for ale
no cause to let his fists fly

she might miss the frantic dash
of clouds across the roiling sky
the creaking howl of the trees
by the paddock's edge

she might even shrug off
the first chilly caress
along the nape of her neck

but she'll shock awake
at the shiver of kisses
on shoulders teased bare

ice tendrils
          trickling
the length of her spine

she might furl tight
try to shake free
but bone-deep she knows
she's already done for

has always been done for

and each time she's flung back
into reliving the maelstrom

demon babe
quickening in her belly
squalling in her arms
tumbling underfoot

lone awake in the cold dark night

a good woman
will tell herself
all she remembers
is the swift pluck into air
the hard jolt back to ground
hair tangled, clothes shredded, skin torn

an honest woman
might own unspoken
the memory of breath
chill on her breasts
the burn of ice
between her thighs

but only a woman
bound for ruination
would dare admit to missing
that knife-lick of pleasure
the constant ache
for its return

JACQUELINE MEZEC

Tattoo

She feels the needle embroidering her skin,
as if her heart is made visible at last.
This one is a rose and dagger because
Love is a beautiful and a dangerous thing.
She is a map of Love's demise,
her skin a pattern book of necromancer art.
Outside in the Frankfurt streets
cars are nudging towards the city's heart.

Locked in the mirror's loveless glance
she remembers her first one, clasped
in a uniformed convict's arms
like some tribal dance, the needle punishing
her dreaming, a Braille of blood
branding her a prostitute, a refugee, a Jew,
this lace-making with her body to carve
the jewelled crimson of a new tattoo.

Sometimes, looking at the tapestry of her veins,
she sees that she has made something after all
of a life lived between the boundaries,
pushing onwards to the last taboo.
She likes to imagine herself lying at rest,
age-marked with dignity, her rose
as fresh as the day it was etched on her skin,
the only beautiful and wholly perfect thing.

Ghost Blanket

You gave me a friendship blanket:
it is beautiful.
You didn't spin the wool yourself
or steep it in earth dyes
which you had crushed with a stone
to blood red, nut brown.
You didn't make a loom from branches
weighted down with pebbles.
Dew didn't seep into it;
it wasn't rinsed in a stream
and laid out in the sun to dry.
It doesn't smell of you and isn't pungent
with the smoke from your fires.
You didn't think of me,
dream dreams of me, as you wove it
your fingers chapped and numb.
Your ancestors didn't blow through it
as it hung, misting their breath into yours.
The pattern doesn't reveal
anything about your people;
there are no stories pricked in with the stitches
no clues to hunting grounds or homes.
You gave me a friendship blanket
in the airport departure hall

and you turned into a bird.

Kolya waiting for the Bird Woman

tiny bird tracks in the snow
in the snow outside his window
little arrows pointing
down the tin roof
like an omen
of a woman coming

Kolya's mother warns him
speaking with a mouth of vinegar
not to marry
not to marry a girl with the feet of a bird
says that women are very cunning
at concealing their bird feet

Anna cascades into the village hall
slips out of her wraps
of marmot and musk rat
dances in her petticoats
around a candle in an ashtray
she dances around a candle
but her feet look normal
out of their fur boots

Kolya's mother fears that
as a tree is sculpted by histories of wind
as a road embodies journeys
as a desert seed holds foreknowledge of rain
so the bird woman hides memories of flight

Anna sings shrill and jubilant
noises from her throat
Anna sings
pours vodka on the hearth to please the spirits
the chimney answers in a cloud of soot
it is cold
she stays the weekend
hibernating
in his bedroom
drinking sweet tea
wrapped in blankets
hibernating
reading poems
laughing saying
that the world isn't made of words

when Anna rises
from her nest of scarves
in lamplight
tattoos on her shoulder look like black lace
tattoos look like black wings
and she leaves to hitch to Moscow
trailing feathers on the lino

after her
his room feels empty
Kolya is frightened
Kolya is frightened that if someone holds him
up to light pouring through the window
they will see through him
they will see his desire to fly

Kolya sings

The Pathologist prepares to send a Valentine

She can deduce much about a man from his heart,
once she has cut it free of his cold body; cleaving
closer than any lover could desire, this solid
geography of flesh opens to her like a map,
colours and shapes hinting whether a life was lived
wantonly and fast or prudently, laboriously, slow.
But here in her cool lab, gatekeeper and high priestess
of clinical ritual, steel instruments can't register
whether a heart ever broke or how much its owner loved,
if at all, or whether he raged passionate to the end
or quietly turned to death.
Back in her warm, cramped flat, she writes her valentine.
The gold-encrusted heart seems naked on white card,
red of artists, crimson, vermilion. Her black
ink words are an opening she isn't sure she wants,
a cut. She can't suppress a fear that, years from now,
her secret will be traced by saliva, a fingerprint,
one solitary, shiny, human hair. Solid as an engine,
her heart will pump blood till its destined end;
whether it soars or sings is for the poets.

DIANE MOORE

déjà vu
Beirut, August 2006

a top-floor room
could be anywhere
a broken guitar
could be anyone's
a bed slept in before
flowers that need watering
hot vapours through
open windows
fragments of glass
the muezzin calling
an old photograph
on the floor

i stand in magenta shadows
think of memory
the chords my fingers touched
pentatonic blues
echoing in a mind
the muezzin calling
our bed still warm
cardamom coffee
an empty watering can
window boxes dripping
onto the pavement
below

The Snail
Chromatic Composition 1953

Wheelchair-bound he scissors
gouache-smeared scraps,
orange feelers

carved from citrus
choppy shapes.
Red and yellow slime

sculpted, pasted,
torn, pinned into
syncopated movement,

the snail-shell unrolling mauve
and black blocks,
intense kinetic whorls

in abstracted nature.
Geometric shards,
logarithmic renewal,

Matisse's penultimate
découpage, infinity
thrust over the edge.

green blood haiku

crumbling into clay,
two september apple trees –
muscled twigs blurring

my filtered vision
over the smudged horizon –
this is the right place

for us to kiss, let
new love add weight to sodden
soil, a confusion

of growth and twitching
antennae. Open branches
tickling our hair, all

within a frameless
future. Wind coyly folding
around a spiral

of brandy leaves.

Not Losing his Marbles

I still see him perched in the armchair, Grandpa,
head cocked like a bird, listening
to my brother's unbroken voice —
can we play marbles?

Know what these are? he billows.
Animated, the years fall away
as he rolls out the marble tale —

1937 champion of St Marks!
Twenty three King Bumblebees —
Won them all, fair and square.

Their yellow/black ribbons
chink against more spheres of expression in the tin —
aventurine cat's eyes, flaming shooter swirls,
cobalt clearies.

He stoops, fingers a corkscrew aggie,
knuckles down to demonstrate a shot,
before his yesteryear self once again
crumples back into the settee.

She wanted it to go blue

Stewing steak strikes the pan
With a hiss.
Spaghetti spews from the packet
Scatters onto

Forgotten coffee
Sends it volcanoing
To the tiles.

Under the knife
Are green chillies.
Pots erupt their blistering liquid.

She yanks the plug
From the mains.

In her scarlet shirt
Her back to the hob

Again she turns her eyes
To the stick she peed on –
The colour unchanged.

Bette Davis

Grandma dreamed
of fifties movie-stardom.
She wanted a perfect blonde bob,
a tiny waist and full skirts,
a loving husband,
a beautiful home
and two wonderful children.

Grandma found
marriage and motherhood
with eight children.
When she died her hands
wore the tenderness of dishwater.

I'll avenge Grandma,
I'll travel back in time
and direct every film.
Bette Davis will be the star.
She'll wear a pencil skirt,
with black patent stilettos
and a cigarette hanging from her red painted lips
as she stares contemptuously at every man.

Green Wax Jacket

Green wax jacket lives in the country
with green fields edged by woolly green hedges.
Green wax jacket has a steady living
with soil, plants and animals for colleagues.
Green wax jacket is the outdoors type
that's where it spends its recreational time.

My lover wore a green wax jacket,
it changed his face.
It added security to his smile
and said his shining eyes were honest.

Green wax jacket has a secret
that only the rain knows.
It's a temptation the rain can't resist,
an adventure course of speedy decline
and inside green wax jacket stays dry.

My lover wore a green wax jacket
when he left.

Peig's Vigil
Peig Sayers 1873-1958

I sit and wait for him to return
like many nights before.
He's with the other one.
Why do I wait?
I stare into the fire and remember
when I saw him first.

In Spring men drink and deliberate
on prospects;
when my turn came I sat,
a dumb witness
to the design of my affairs,
looking up timidly
at his wise young face
and the twitching sinews
of his broad shoulders and arms.
I pledged to myself then
to make him a good wife.
Later, I tasted her salt on his lips,
I knew it was her breath
that wizened his face
and the labour of hauling
the bounties beneath her skirts
that defined his limbs.

She is a lover with no allegiance,
she swells to the sun
and the mirror moonlight,
and raises her frock to the wind
flaunting the froth of her underclothes.
She has a ceaseless appetite

that has taken many,
even when she has shaded
his lips with her hue
she will swallow more.

CHUMA NWOKOLO

Edge of Extinction

In vain does this sphincter
slow the species' final slide
into the flood beyond.

In the meantime does this museum
play mausoleum to these ghosts that
pass the aeons of their sentence waiting,
waiting for you.

I am snatch of language lost,
in the echo of caves.

I am song infused in
fossils flown the coop.

Birds that once migrated seas
in search of sun
have now transmigrated worlds
and won't return.

I am the broken valve
through whom a world deflates.

Wait long enough in the
slipstream of my dreams
and you will hear again,
birdsong from fossil realms.

Songs for chiming at a rising sun,
now sulk in memorial galleries.

I am a surprised terracotta mask
gapes at comedy gone sour.

I am a runic stone
relates a victory gone stale.

I am the valve incontinent
feeds a wailing wind the
flatulence of human histories.

Wait, and you will hear again,
the stomp of mammoth herd,
the shriek of winged turtle …
and old laughter,
as an extinct tribesman from an antique culture tells,
in a vanished tongue,
a sublime joke whose punchline you will never catch.

The Creature Longer than a Mile

They think I'm deaf and dumb,
a destitute whose last legs failed
on Mordia's stony heath.
They'll never know.
The things I've seen!
You'll have to climb the Mordia Range at dawn.
You'll have to trek the four clans on the crest.
You then must ford the Kamson Stream
and walk twelve miles downstream –
if I knew an easier way, I'd say it, no?

Leave the stream at her delta, yes?
Young girls will smile and hawk
fried snails in luscious onion rings,
but Death lurks here in lust.
Go on.

There's a boatman there who won't take fees –
but do reject his gin too, yes?
Cross with the gods' boatman.
It will be swiftly night,
but the moon is always full in Kamson Gorge.
You will find yourself by
The-Baobab-that-Hastens-Night;
& you will see their graves:
the grave of my speech, and
the grave of my hearing too.
You'll see them there.

And as you raise your eyes
you'll see his haunches
and the wonder of his swishing tail.
You then must thwart the modern lure
to find & photograph,
to be the first,
to culture fame …
you must ignore the wonder of
The Creature Longer than a Mile.

But you won't, will you?
You are Modern Man.
You must be the fastest,
richest, wisest, first.
Yesterday saw the moon-shadow
at the bottom of the lake,
and Today wears a new title:
'Discoverer of the Moon'.
You will trail the curve of his furry flank
to demystify his face.
You will spend your next decade
on that next mile.

Then you will make your broken way back,
where, by The-Baobab-that-Hastens-Night,
you will find two further graves.

They will think you are deaf and dumb,
a destitute, but they'll never know.
Will they?

Managing Catastrophe

chaga-chaga. Curious how that morning passed;
there was not time enough to think it through.
What with the dozen desperate things to do:
her sullen staff and cluttered desk; what with
the inventories, the calls, the old accounts,
that morning's tension was a swollen boil,
its crisis was the ague, they sapped her will —
the halting marriage to bring to a head,
the juggling act with bills and summonses …
she had barely strength enough to rise from bed.
How that morning passed was truly strange.

At first, she lay there somnolent and stunned.
Another snatch of sleep seemed just the thing
to ease the band encasing her temples.
But she was strong. She steeled herself.
Her crises called for deeds, not sleep.
So she fetched the cream cake and the lemon tea;
with grim resolve, she did a crossword quiz.
She poured another cup. She cut a slice.
She watched TV … the morning passed.
She had foiled catastrophe with a pot of tea.
She sipped some more. *chaga-chaga*.
The train bore down upon her picnic on the rails.
She tuned it out fiercely, thinking all the while,
'I *really* must get up and grapple life …'
Knowing all the while,
with certainty steeped in old despair,
that she only had strength
enough for one more cup of lemon tea.

Prayer before Flight

after Louis Macneice

I'm about to fly, so help me.

May the heaven-bound youth with the
lust for virgins miss my flight.
when the prodding wand comes my way
let it beep briefly, and be
gone

Give me this day
panties like a crab's carapace,
shield me from the scanner with the voyeur eye;
dress me in corsets for coarse hands and
in bras to brace me for the small room
where they queue with a fiat
to grope
me

Kill us foxes for our furs,
bulls for our belts &
alligators for the shoes on that flight –
and may the soles on all shoes on that plane
be true wood

May the pops on that flight
spill champagne and
no more

I am *hijabed*, have mercy.
I lack grace under grief:
do not profile me with the Palestinian beard,

the Arab-sounding name, or the youth from Lagos.
may my sufferings be brief.
let the cup of Iraqi-accented Urdu-speaking men from Yemen
pass by me.

I am scared,
bung me up.
constipate me when I eat.
insulate me from the long toilet call
on that ten-hour-trip in the skies.

Grant me short, dreamless sleep when I doze.
seat the spy on the plane far from me.
& if I mutter in my sleep,
may the words 'bomb' and 'terror'
not be said

Bless me with a pilot that has learnt how to take-off
and land, and may your kingdom come
(not today).

LINDA ROSE PARKES

Muses of the Shower Room

They're there behind the shower curtain,
giving off headiness of rose, the calm
of geranium mingled with salt of a fresh swim.

Snuck under the bra of a tankini is a seaweed tendril.
What more to say? Yet still they shadow the quiet of distance:
when I'm going for a pee or standing on a chair

to fix a light bulb, they insist on holding to the subject
of how the tide has reached the shingle line, dusk breezing
into the bay, asking only that the waves break at the edge

of consonance, that vowels be bestowed with the soughing
quality of the near-drowned. Of syntax they desire
an expansiveness, a oneness between body

of text and their own fluent strokes.
What if I can't convey the rocky escarpments, shifting
light and breaking surfaces? Or if I fail

in the sludge between words to suggest the power
of the submerged narrative: love's losses
and growing old? Will they pursue me until the work

is done; until they, untouched by winter approaching,
bask in the shored-up waters of the page?
But I hear them now – emerging from the sea and heading

for the shower room ... trailing their towels along the sand-
swilled floor! Yes, I can feel the pummelling all down
their spines, taste the fragrance lapping their silhouettes.

The U-Boat Kapitän summoned by Pegasus

Every night I was looking for a sign
that I could sleep without dreams
of broken men – I watched the enemy

captain stroll on the bridge, a streak
of bubbles tracking the torpedo,
stokers, grooms storming the hatchways,

and wedged stall upon stall,
the rearing, slipping horses
bound for the Front.

I crammed my eyes with stars
in the hope of a day worth the trouble
of my ablutions, the wearing of a good tie.

But stranded nightly in my backyard,
I was summoned by ghosts:
the bay mare quivering

in the horse star constellation,
the lunging deeps of her eyes
as she attempted to swim,

the white stallion leaping
over the berthing rail –
when I saw him land – O *mein gott!*

in a full-laden boat, I shut down
the periscope,
shouted orders to dive.

Finally run aground, in slippers and bathrobe,
I kneel to Pegasus, under the weight
of what I've done. Tonight,

inside the whinnying dark,
gashing hooves, veering flanks,
sweeping necks of arched muscle

come to perfect rest. And lifting
from the blood and smoke,
the mangled souls rise.

Swimming Out
for Carole

No, it wasn't wise to strip off,
give herself over
to the waves slapping
her knees and then her breasts
before she lunged
into the steeply-
shelving ocean
in late summer's emptied bay
where the kiosk
flapped its ripped
awning and the slipway
merged into the hill
studded with conifers
and crumbling cliff.

But so often the wind
had pummelled her windows
and salt stained the glass. Now finally
she was pushing out
from a paint-flaked,
middle-aging house
of dust-scorched roses.
If she made it beyond
the hook of fear,
success would surf her
past the lowering
rocks and if her strokes
stalled she'd learn to float
until the creases in her breath
dissolved and it was only
the brine in her veins
which owned her –

her spirit rising
like Leviathan,
eyes like eyelids
of the morning.

Dawdling Boy
picks up
Momentum
for Samuel

Knees splayed under low-slung handlebars
        his gangly, calf-like limbs bridled –
    the pent-up grace
        of a boy who lists
    when he walks

Half-hidden behind a wildflower bank
    a cow reared her head
 and made to kiss him:
        he veered –
                nearly lost
            balance
    righted himself
 on his short saddle …
    the elegance of the near thing

She'd heard him of course
        the ticking of his wheels
 in her nasal world could sniff
    his presence, the sweet-warm sweat
 of young skin – her calf
        not full-weaned
 from her wet-lick
        corralling tongue

But the calf
        cycles on
    pedalling faster
        now faster
 racing himself
            against

himself past the flood-green
fields, the leafing
trees holding the bend
boy
as boy
propelled
by space and time

her eyes still following

Nanny's Coffee

Every young girl crazy with pain
would find solace in Nanny's roomy girth,
the thick aroma of exhortations
to put some blood back in the veins

by drinking *le bon café, noir et sucré.*
Now, if you were Antigone,
this coffee might throw the tale
off course, pulling you to the roof

of your mouth, the needy furze
at the back of the tongue.
With coffee warming in the hearth,
you could find yourself starting

to be lulled by the sight of the steam,
the sound of Nanny's voice,
feel of her housecoat pressed
to your cheek. For you, hope never has fled

that far — so far you couldn't call it back
with the thought of a party, a new dress,
the handsome bloke who's bound
to glance your way.

But imagine: the flagstones, winter and cold,
cold morning after days without sleep;
your rebel brother rotting on the road
and no one else to bury him against the king's edict.

Our heroine knows she has no choice
but to be entombed with him.
Le sale espoir! This kidding oneself.
And look at Nanny –

all love and anguish as she bellows
the fire, grabs the pot. You can taste
her sweat from where you're sitting
as daybreak filters through the room.

Her roughly swept back hair falls
loose over one eye and she pushes it
roughly behind her ear.
No thoughts but for Antigone;

that stubborn girl will break her heart.
But no – it must not come to that!
Drink, ma petite, come warm yourself!
Let sleep gloss over ugly times. What's done is done.

Oligohydramnios

It was my first dead body,
And the first I'd abetted.
Swaddled and coddled in a hospital towel.
We had four hours, with the tang of iron,
Salted collars, dilute tea, flat flattened sandwiches and
A featherweight bundle, back, fro, back and fro,
Over a beat of flamenco.

It was an unblameable loss, a mugging of potential
With no footpad to pursue, no crusade to valve it off.
It was slim elongated fingers tipped with tight, tiny nails
Which did not stir, for all the watching.
It was a red bean heart which only beat on screen.
An intricate working theory, a genderless possibility,
A warming idea, cooling down.

It was subconscious plans, uncounted, bobbing up,
Belly up, sprinkling the compass point,
Had to keep eyes horizoned as they nuzzled round.
And us becalmed.
And around the quiet reminders of an ache not gone to rest,
Far beyond our ability to curse.

It was sudden membership to a covert grief,
Invitations to the group Morsed on tapped doors,
Quiet people there, knowing what not to say.
It was surprising: the desolation in the weekly shop,
The kryptonite of expectant women,
The moppet's lethal smile, a midnight solar plexus lurching,
A turvy wolf inside, clawing out.

It was all too close to the surface.
It was a rejection of comfort, an urge to rage.
A gloom that would not stay in its box.
It was something that mattered. It matters still; will.
It was a miracle removed.

ADAM PERCHARD

A Voice from the Undergrowth

I don't know what I think,
down here in the undergrowth.
There are leaves the colour of peaches.
An air full of rustles,
everywhere twig-brittle browns and silvers and …
our bones become the mulch,
and sometimes we don't know –
whether we step on twigs or ribs,
femurs … beneath our wet, succulent flesh
we are a fragile network of twigs.
Our rodent-bird bodies are so fragile
when we move quickly it's a wonder we don't snap.
Down here the smells of growth and decay have never been
so close.
We live in the smell of death. Sh-h-h-
can you hear us? We skitter in the bark.

Our feet look like they were added on at the last minute;
more corporeal than the rest of us,
you could become obsessed with their delicious pinkness
amongst the faun.

Forty-One years in the same House

Do you see this dust?
The dust which hovers here
                    (made motes of light by the old and viscous sun)
so lightly
how it dances when your hand passes through …
do you see?

It is mostly our skincells.
We are settling on you like a soft rain.

We danced down that line of carpet,
rooms flashing past, flushed with the smell of lilac –
we remember doorframes only as streaking shadows.
Tears, laughter, vomit,
we cannot find the difference now.

We are only the brass lion-head handles on the wardrobe:
we mouth our shining rings and watch
as you grow and fade and grow
and fade.

At Brandfold

Tim, my mum's brother, has died.
His freckles are painted in the loft
in faded watercolour greys
next to my grandmother's skirts.

I leaf through them
like wilted peony petals
in the jaw-strong box
under the eaves

and am alive
amongst their mothballed scent.

Remembered energy
kindles in my throat
or stomach-wall
every now and then

when I breathe their dust.

MARTIN PORTER

a dripping tap
Marilyn in New York

… elongated,
  necking to almost wasp waisted thinness,
'till it releases the elegant gem, splitting sunlight
  into a blaze of red green blue gone
  and impacts with ear jarring sound, leaps up again,
  beautiful, as a spreading crown and
  ebbs away.

  The continual noise has awoken her, so
  Marilyn moves to the faucet where
  another drop has begun to swell. She watches
  as it slowly builds from tiny pimple to
  full grown boil, sees her own reflection in
  its full grown curvature, looks
  as the imaged phantom tumbles
  into the sink.

  She knows Arthur will return home soon and
  the steady fall will be no longer hers.
  In the shining chrome she sees herself reach forward,
  her own distorted hand now hides her body,
  and she withdraws to stare again, sighs, looks up
  to see if she is there, still in control, still in the centre, and
  the drop emerges, elongated …

My Lover is a Rainstorm

My lover is a thunderstorm
Grey ripples flickering
Tiny landscapes of stone
Upright, steadfast

And as I watch
My lover paints calligraphy
An illuminated landscape shrunken
waves of jointed, colourless bamboo
watery characters in
upright folds
with all the meaning of

The vacuum
Of the landscape words.

And I say Help me
I am outside, cold and wet

Drenched in chill fascination,
Rattling hollow spaces between drops
Distilling the dews of bronchial chambers.

Like the pine
I grasp the cliff
Dripping.

The morning sun
Drives my lover spectral
from my bed
fleeing colour
rising in

Waves breaking over the hills
Silver sky silver water
Silver blues and greys
Silver greys, off-whites and almost black

Nothingness
as firm as the landscape it holds

And I say Help me, I am
bewildered, chilled
to the heart.

I know my lover from
Snatched glimpses through the grasses,

Snatched glimpses through the mist.

ALEX RICE

The Razor Fish Bowl

I'm ten and crouching
at a keyhole,
barefoot on moist sand;
and with a pinch of salt – an unexpected
briny squirt,
the razor fish, clammy
in my hand, is pale, penile
and plump – folded in a brittle shell. I squint
into the lens; and before the click
of a shutter unspools
me into adulthood to stare
back, we've plucked
over a hundred from their burrows,
as if the sea's tongue had licked
them deep inside …
Next morning I peer
into the bay
of the casserole bowl
to find that glass-eyed farmer
Uncle Arthur, has eaten all our catch
for breakfast!

Choreographed, the tide strips
into channels. Dad's in my veins
and we sprint
like schoolboys between reefs,
water dimpling as we tread,
lost to everything but glancing
mullet, that flick and flash
chasing through pockets.
We plunge into the sea's skirts
breasting the waves before the beach
becomes a white gash
against dark sky. I retrace my steps
over a cache of limpet rings,
hearing the pitch and toss
of Dad's laugh.

night flights

a still house
on a still night
a linen sigh
of restless sleep

a gentle pad downstairs
a glass of water
a cat purrs
and is fed at this odd hour

of silence
                stars
                        and moon

how much comfort is there
                                in a glass of water?
how much meaning
                        going back to bed?

when we are normal in the morning
swept along in the family rush
who will remember

the stars
        the silence
                and the moon
pressing on the window

and the night flights

coming home to land?

femme fatale

she kept his balls in her bag.
she thought he could not be trusted.
perhaps she was right.

he left her for somebody, younger.
too young even to own
a handbag?

but yesterday she found them again,
slid beneath the oose
under a discarded lipstick:

two little eggs,
the size of a plover's,
but marble white.

pinching one delicately,
between forefinger and thumb,
she slipped it into her mouth;

mirror smooth,
she coddled it
on her thick, wet, tongue.

far away,
on a beach in Malaga,
he shuddered.

'just someone
           walking over my grave',
he said.

patron saint

We spent the morning in Amalfi.
I wandered round in the basilica,
stopped beside St Andrew's tomb.
I thought I'd light a candle for my father.
He was a simple man, it seemed
a simple thing to do.

His hard religion banned the use of ornament,
or ancient tongue, or ritual to form
its simple truths.
He would have told me
this was idolatry,

but I observe the local customs and move on.
Love is such a fearsome thing to say.

sea gardener

I passed an old man
on the shore today,

heaping mounds of vraic
onto a rickety hand cart.

forkfuls of leaf slapping
limbs of fleshy succulent,

tangling and splaying,
like the blackened bodies of the drowned.

he paused, slicked back a smile, sank
lustrous tines into

a sodden mass at his feet.
good gardening weather, we agreed.

then, drawing breath,
he returned to his gleaning,

careless as the sea.

forced spring

cotils

potato fields
in flanks and slopes

are wrapped in polythene
to catch the warmth

to work the soil
force an early crop

the dark heart of the island
untouchable beneath

this smooth translucence
for weeks the grey sky

floods the earth
until the skin is split

and musky scents escape
and hooded figures jackknife

across the landscape
clawing the swollen tubers

free

SHAUN SHACKLETON

100 to 1 to win minus Tax

A tear of paper with a sum on,
where he worked out the winnings
of an imaginary bet,
is all I have left of my father.
No watch, no heirloom
no pillow-sunk last words,
just blue biro on a corner ripped from The Sun.
It's where nothing becomes everything
and everything becomes nothing again.

Rose Cottage

I wondered how many had taken this trip,
down the staff-only service stairs,
along the maintenance corridor with the tiles missing
making a chessboard floor of concrete and linoleum,
the long ceiling of pipes and wires
stopped at night like an artery system,
then into the cold room with the metal drawers
next to the chapel of quiet wood and wilting carnations.
For me, it was my first; for you, your first and last.
Two days old and you never once opened your eyes.
I didn't know anything then, that was my job,
but I could've told you that they were blue.
They are always blue.

Rose Cottage is hospital porter code for a death on a ward

To Bradford, Leeds and beyond

In science labs
with gas taps
in the benches
we found out that up the fields
they were laming horses
with broken glass again.

Cant and Matlock
were taken away
by police van
for murder:
school uniforms suddenly
like suits.

And she slipped me
her strawberry tongue
at the disco. Some of her toenails
left unpainted
like great cities
waiting to be built.

The broken Road

crows swarm
the carcass of a rabbit,
plucking its heart
through the harp
of its ribcage.

the fort is sunk
    swallowed by the
            spike and tip
        of gorse,
the battlements
granite teeth
bared at the sea.
every window is
meshed in steel
as though the walls
are made of garnet,
but inside the rooms
are empty as quarries.

I lift a stone from the road,
throw it,
and close my eyes.

my father has been dying
now for a year.

I hear the stone land
in the dam of my stomach,
sending ripples
to the shores of toestubs
and fingertips:

if I can find it
among all the others
he won't go today.

Recherché

Z Cars and Zabaglione
warming on a telly's
glowing valves.

The wipers clear a windscreen drenched with headlights,
the white line in the darkness dazzles.
A familiar drive, M23 to Brighton,
a comfortable supper
just me and Dad.

Crème brulée, béarnaise sauce,
all perfected in the double boiler –
André Simon, Larousse.

I ring the doorbell,
peer through the stained glass.

In the small acrid kitchen
his eyes flicker, pale and rheumy,

I glance into a pan
where pasta, sauce less,
turns brown
within an inch of water.

Zuppa Inglese

Its whipped cream snowy surface
rivalled Christmas.
Whistling carols after midnight mass,
he'd stir a second custard batch.
An annual affair –
my father's trifle.

Slivered almonds adorned
its surface like new teeth:
angelica, cherries and amoretti.

By the day of the three French hens,
its contours a massive landslide after rain,
the almonds now like fallen gravestones
on collapsing slopes.

The Decisive Moment

He aims.
Prepares to
shoot
through the diminutive
hotel window.

Outside, gyrating
swifts, whirl
spin, dip and hurtle.

Babbling television,
the filling bath, rush hour traffic.
He studies the square below.

Amber light honey-glows the people,
purposeful bees, outside an active hive.
A toddler clasps an adult's hand.
Nearby a woman, shackled
to her backpack
as a snail to its shell.

The room breathes cool.
Scented steam saturates the wilting city air.
The bath tap ticking drips,
the commentary blathers on:
suicide, bombers, casualties.

He scans his digital images.
An upturned face
her clammy skin
and soaring pulse
unnoticed.

Nothing captured there.
He reaches for the camera's dustbin sign.
Delete. Delete. *Delete* …

As one
they press.

NATHAN THOMPSON

the magic study of happiness

following your example   tomorrow
I brighten like flowers opening a book
with the discovery of more flowers

                                         colours to play
in the general direction of being in love accidentally
cooling anemones in rock-pools   we have lived
yesterdays beside an ocean   following the creek
on sunny mornings

                              should I be writing this for you
I'm not sure   some gifts are unwanted but

to see summer from a broad perspective of winter
big things flecked in your corneas

                                 dappled mill ponds

where
white elephants swish off a dusty day
emerging bright stars at an appropriate distance

I imitate you like a train of shadows
like a cat pulling backwards on its lead
like   'the angel knows everything   every second counts
fasten your seatbelt   we're leaving'

here are all the vines entangled
when a ray of light moves me
I will expire on the moss

to fail to learn would be   emphatic
        'if only I had ancestors   I would make gold and
your remedies'

Pulling on a Jersey we walked beyond Sunset

I am tired of small ideas and grandiose statements. I am tired
of the moon coming up like a phosphorescent mushroom over
your incompetence and unwillingness to love. Tomorrow there
will be a different harbour through which to look from your
desert island at glass-lolly skyscrapers under a single palm.

All this talk of height. You don't really think that being close
to someone makes you more aware of them? Well do you? If I
am addressing you, you must be far enough away to write me a
letter. I shall look forward to it. You will correct my grammars
of error, returning the postcards I sent pocked with red ink like
consumptive spit in sawdust.

'Thinking of an ideal poem is close to writing an ideal poem.
In this respect it resembles horticulture or investment banking,'
you say. I am always grateful for your advice. As the credits roll I
put on the kettle while you snore in a distant armchair, bereft of
syntax. You resemble nothing so much as the hollowed insides
of a house contemplating politics.

'But political poems are meant to rhyme,' you say, 'don't you
know that?' I shake my head sadly as a rose born out of season.
You will always find a haven here with me, my love.

news from the hill

getting the sun always right   fluctuations
it is noon-time in the tropics
                                  here it is
almost intimate   half light differentiating
love from lovers in a bare room

the children sleep   mountains dance
refusing any move to point up
towards moments seen through indifference

the moon on the other hand is very high   imagining
something
other than what it already is   an obsessive
diet of cow juice chugging dim engines
over a horizon of hurt professors

this is our twenty eight days to three six five
wandering through a hall of mirrors

as though to pass the same street a thousand times
seems the real thing   you didn't see him / her
also comparing simple

SAMUEL THOMPSON

Echoes from the Beach

Over corrugated sands
Sea water runs in the morning tide.
Weed logged nets hang
From crusted fishing posts
And ripple; low wind dies across the shore.

Over female ribs, purple
Blood runs chill under a downtown moon.
Later bright lights;
Masked nurses sigh and turn
To watch the cardiogram rise and fall.

Three Western Poems

Ogden, Utah

Fork closed round the battle
mountain the same old cut

into many wests our plans
to hide the book cliffs

abandoned in the salt flats if
it rains tonight in Reno we

must do what they did
before that's be mapped last

Elko, Nevada

Rush to choke upon
the next west no

being no negation
we cannot handle

touches upon wood
for water the passion

I put here undersold
reflected in the light

of the latest land
purchase

Price, Utah

It's the last stratum
the rancher owns though

it may be the time it took
to get so far up also

belongs to him. The total
gradient of accumulation, the

steady shift of towns
amongst Carbon County

flats, sometime salt sometime
sand. Arrival in the empty

frequency to lead the
ghost town on

mountain time the hour
told by foot she said it's

near enough to walk

Ici d'ailleurs

the day hides
the stone, serial
relation to the
home is belonging, the hardly visible
binary formation floods
the border with dark red
wood marking the frontier
with its guts, whose day
hides the stone & who will hold it
together? upon the clearing weather
we are more than
all difference that could occur &
the things mentioned are
the things themselves, split
up into the heavy liquid which
seems beautiful & demands care

Lakes of the Rub' al Khali

heat. weight lifts away from the mass
flaps at the feet as the full
technicolour encounter splays
the light sensitive
tissue, we will hurt

the ruin until beginning
appears as late death to tilt
the crowd now warming up

the coordinate with stiff rubbed
hands along the sand, the half-furnished
path to dream demand we boil on or
are edited out like water, this especially good
for the end we're getting all lumped up for
tomorrow he says he was
for the new day the furthest light
we can see & the tissue, of course
it's grey and
they face it too, tomorrow, the trembling
hand with the hole in it, but

tonight, fire! & morning
we're not even
in for it, trailing the desert inside
our favourite things the ones
we love with
the holes in them, boiled straight
to love in mirage for first light
eye-locked it starts
here, its fresh slip

NOTES ON CONTRIBUTORS

ROBERT ANDERSON is a painter, writer and performance artist, born in Jersey and currently working in New York.

ALASTAIR BEST is a painter. He has also been a magazine editor, university lecturer and writer on architecture and design. He was born and now lives in Jersey.

LIVIA BLUECHER is a great granddaughter of the Prussian Prince Blucher who became tenant of Herm in 1892. She now lives in Guernsey and has published travel writing, poetry and short fiction in local magazines in the US and UK. Her poems were recently chosen for the Pens and Lens exhibition, sponsored by the Guernsey Arts Commission and for the island's Poetry on the Buses scheme.

SHARON CHAMPION was born and educated in Jersey and in 2004 obtained a BA (Hons) from the Open University. She won the Channel Islands' Writers' competition in 2008. She currently works at the Jersey Women's Refuge as a residential support worker.

SIMON CROWCROFT has lived and worked in Jersey for most of his life. He was elected to the States (the island's Parliament) in 1996. Following the injury of his son in a road traffic incident he wrote Mean Streets, a pamphlet of poems about the impact of the motor car. Compulsory Showers won third prize in the Bridport competition of 2001 and he has won the Jersey Evening Post Literary Competition three times. He also writes plays, including The Last Voyage of Philip d'Auvergne, which was commissioned by the Jersey Youth Theatre in 2005.

RICHARD FLEMING was born in Northern Ireland but moved to the Channel Islands 16 years ago. He is a member of the Guernsey Arts Commission and is currently co-organiser of the Poetry on the Buses scheme. His collection, The Man Who Landed: a Guernsey double is available on amazon.com.

CAROL GAUDION was born in Jersey, and apart from short spells in the UK has lived on the island most of her life.

MARTIN GREENE is a musician, performance artist and occasional poet whose influences include Robert Lowell and John Berryman.

JULIETTE HART has been published in six Jersey Arts Trust anthologies, four anthologies published by Leaf Books and by Magma magazine. She was born in Jersey to parents who lived on the island during the German occupation.

BARBARA JOYNER has published Single Supplement, a memoir of poems and short stories. At the age of 78 she is currently working on her first novel.

ALAN JONES was born in Jersey, educated at Bristol and London universities and was head of English at Hautlieu School. He has been runner-up in several UK poetry competitions, and twice won the Jersey Evening Post Writing competition.

CHRISTINE JOURNEAUX has lived in Jersey for the past 40 years but her writing often evokes childhood memories of family life on an Oxfordshire farm.

JUDY MANTLE was born and brought up in Jersey. She returned to the island in 1979 after studying and teaching in England, France and Canada.

PENELOPE MCGUIRE is a writer and photographer who has written extensively on architecture, town planning and design for the national and international press.

NICKY MESCH was born in Jersey, studied Chinese and French at the Polytechnic of Central London and lived in Nanjing, London and Hong Kong before returning to Jersey in 1997. Her work has appeared in Magma and the Interpreter's House as well as in anthologies such as Outbox & other poems (*Leaf Books*) and In the Telling (*Cinnamon Press*).

JACQUELINE MEZEC is Jersey born of Breton parentage. Her poems have won prizes in competitions organised by the Jersey Arts Trust, Jersey Evening Post, Jersey Eisteddfod and the Kent and Sussex Poetry Society. She has undertaken commissions for the Jersey Evening Post, Holocaust Memorial Day and the 25th anniversary celebrations of the Jersey Arts Centre. Her short screen play Breathe was the winner of Jersey's first scriptwriting competition and the film was premiered at the Branchage International Film Festival.

DIANE MOORE was born in Jersey and studied modern languages and literature at a number of British and European universities, specialising in French, German and Norwegian. She has published poetry and literary articles in several magazines, and has also written a number of plays and non-fiction books, the most recent, Deo Gratias focussing on the history of the French Catholic church in Jersey since the French Revolution.

SANDRA NOEL was born in Jersey. Her work was published in the Channel Islands' anthology 2008, and a short story won the Jack Higgins trophy in the literary section of the 2010 Jersey Eisteddfod.

HAZEL NOLAN is Irish and has lived in Jersey since 1996. She studied Creative Writing at University of Glamorgan in Wales. While there she was published in 3 issues of the University's Daps Magazine and worked on the editorial team for the magazine for a year. She is currently focusing on her fiction writing.

CHUMA NWOKOLO was called to the bar in 1984. He has worked for the Legal Aid Council and was managing partner of C&G Chambers, Lagos. He was writer in residence at the Ashmolean Museum and chairman of Leys Newspapers, Oxford. He is publisher of African Writing magazine. His novels include Diaries of a Dead African (2003) and he has published a collection of poems, Memories of Stone. When living in Guernsey he convened, in 2009, Gustavus Guernsey, an African writers' mini-festival for the Channel Islands.

LINDA ROSE PARKES was born in Jersey and studied Literature at the University of East Anglia. Her full length collections, *The Usher's Torch* (2005) and *Night Horses* (2010) were published by Hearing Eye. She has often performed alongside musicians and also writes song lyrics.

RICHARD PEDLEY is an actor and lawyer.

ADAM PERCHARD spent much of his childhood in India, and moved to Jersey at the age of 15. He won joint first prize in the Channel Islands Writers' competition 2008. He read English at Oxford and York universities and is working on a PhD in 18th century and post-colonial literature.

MARTIN PORTER was born in Jersey and now lives in New Zealand. He studied astro-physics, specialising in high energy cosmic radiation, before returning to Jersey to teach. He won the poetry section of the Channel Islands Writers' competition in 2005.

ALEX RICE studied Philosophy at Kent University and now lives and works in Jersey, teaching English as a foreign language.

COLIN SCOTT trained as an actor in Glasgow and Paris before switching to writing. His work has appeared in the Edinburgh Fringe, London's West End and BBC Radio 4. He is part of Off The Rock, a new theatrical venture, based in Jersey.

SHAUN SHACKLETON was born in Guernsey, but grew up in Keighley, West Yorkshire. He has worked variously as a forklift driver, spray painter, postman, labourer and gravedigger and currently works for the Guernsey Press.

PIPPA SIMPSON portrays her ideas in glass, drawing, painting and poetry. She has had several solo exhibitions at the Jersey Arts Centre and in 2008 held an exhibition at Durrell (Jersey's zoo) on the theme of extinct animals.

NATHAN THOMPSON is the author of three collections of poetry: The Arboretum Towards the Beginning (Shearsman 2008); Holes in the Map (Oystercatcher 2010); and A Haunting (Gratton Street Irregulars 2010). Nathan lived in Jersey from 2007 to 2010 and ran the poAttic reading series at Jersey's Opera House.

SAMUEL THOMPSON's poetry has appeared in several British and American publications and he has broadcast his poetry on BBC Radio. Previous volumes include Church Poems and Where Home Was, both published by the Saumarez Press, Guernsey. He and his family now live in Majorca.

TOMAS WEBER was born in Jersey. His first pamphlet, The Small Stones was published in 2009 with Perdika Press. His work has been published in many poetry magazines and he has read his poems in Cambridge, London, Oxford and Montevideo. His work will shortly be appearing in a new anthology of modernist British poetry. He is currently a student at Cambridge University, where he is collaborating on a translation into French of the American poet John Wieners.

PUBLISHER'S ACKNOWLEDGEMENTS

JULIETTE HART
Mirror, Signal, Manoeuvre (*Leaf Books*),
A single returns on the Gatwick Express (*Magma*)

NICKY MESCH
Testing her Metal and Death of a Unicorn (*Cinnamon Press*)

LINDA ROSE PARKES
Muses of the Shower Room (*poetry tREnD, English-German translation*),
The U-Boat Kapitan summoned by Pegasus (*Leaf Garden Press*),
Swimming Out and Dawdling Boy picks up Momentum
(*Night Horses: Hearing Eye*),
Nanny's Coffee (*Leviathan Quarterly*)

SHAUN SHACKLETON
The Broken Road (Joint Winner of the Channel Islands Writers'
Competition 2005 and entered for the Forward Prize 2005)

NATHAN THOMPSON
The Magic Study of Happiness and News from the Hill
(*Stride Magazine*)

TOMAS WEBER
Three Western Poems, Ici D'ailleurs and Lakes of the Rub'al Khali
(*Better than language: Ganzfeld Press*)